Early Diesels in the East Midlands

No. 37: **TOTON**

Pictures by **DON BEECROFT & DAVID DALTON**

Copyright Book Law Publications 2012
ISBN 978-1-907094-28-6

INTRODUCTION

During the transition years from steam to diesel motive power, the area of British Railways centred around Toton in the East Midlands was to benefit from investment in a new, purpose built, diesel depot which was reputedly the largest such establishment in Western Europe. The area eventually became the Nottingham Division of BR which effectively covered vast tracts of the counties of Nottinghamshire, Derbyshire and Leicestershire. It was no coincidence that the boundaries of all three shires contained within them much of the remaining reserves of the coalfields which had been worked for over a century prior to the implementation of BR's Modernisation Plan in 1955. Bisecting the centre of the newly created Division was the Midland Main Line which, besides being a major artery for the coal traffic originating within the Division, was the principal passenger route from the north and east midlands to the Capital. The major population centre within the Division was the City of Nottingham which had seen much so-called rationalisation of its railway infrastructure during the period of the 'transition' and afterwards. It effectively lost a major trunk railway (Britain's 'Last Main Line' the Great Central) and much of its local network finishing up more or less from where it began at the start of the Railway Age.

This album has been compiled to hopefully reflect, with some degree of diversity, the years in question. Illustrations vary from those depicting locomotives on shed and in works, to trains in the urban and semi-rural landscape.

Although not a native of the area, this 'compiler' has drawn on the services of 'local people' to add, examine, correct, and bless the various facts and figures used in the captions. Amongst those I would like to thank for their contributions are Bill Taylor, Dave Paylor and Hayden Reed. However, two other people have worked so hard on this project that their names should have been on the cover too. What started as a simple proof reading job turned into an investigative project wherever doubt raised its head – and it did; midnight oil was burnt by the gallon (or is that litres now?) and electronic mail came into its own. So, to Ian Trivett and Neill Fisher, I give many thanks to you both for showing not just your enthusiasm but also diligence, knowledge, patience and a sense of humour which certainly made the whole thing a pleasure.

Cover Picture (See Page 52)

(previous page) **It is April 1975, and we are at the site of Stapleford and Sandiacre station (closed 2nd January 1967), in the shadow of the A52 dual-carriageway road bridge, as 45017 (ex D23) trundles across the pointwork at the northern boundary of Toton yard with a Down empty MGR train bound for one of the collieries further north. The train would be bound for one of those collieries not equipped with a rapid loading bunker, more than likely a 'pad' comprising a long concrete strip with attendant mechanical front-loading shovel which would fill the stationery train. Not being equipped with slow speed control (SSC), the 'Peaks' could not haul the MGR trains at the required half a mile per hour beneath the colliery loading bunkers. *D.H.Beecroft.***

Printed and bound by The Amadeus Press, Cleckheaton, West Yorkshire
First published in the United Kingdom by Book Law Publications, 382 Carlton Hill, Nottingham, NG4 1JA

With the evening sun highlighting the landscape, a Sheffield based Brush Type 2, D5817, steadily climbs the 1 in 290 gradient as it heads north along the Erewash valley main line with an iron stone train in June 1966. We are situated at Shipley Gate, between Langley Mill to the north and Bennerley viaduct, which was just round the bend leading off the top right of the picture. A footbridge which crosses the railway at this point affords not only views such as this but also distant views of trains on the aforementioned ex-GN route from Nottingham to Derby but also on the former GN line to Pinxton which ran parallel with the MR Erewash line as far as Pye Bridge. The viaduct - also known as Forty Bridges - serving the latter line, is just below the horizon above the roof of the diesel. Of course in June 1966 all that was about to change as the GN routes were to close at the end of the year, although the section for a few miles west of Bagthorpe Junction remained open for a couple more years so that iron ore trains travelling along the former Great Central route through Nottingham, could service the Stanton Ironworks situated about four miles south of this location. The ironstone traffic depicted here originated from quarries in either Leicestershire or Northamptonshire. The destination of train 8E55, a daily evening working, was most likely the Stanton & Staveley works at Staveley near Chesterfield. *D.H.Beecroft.*

The following evening, and right on time, the loaded iron ore train 8E55 makes its way north again but with different motive power in the shape of two newly-delivered Beyer, Peacock-built Sulzer Type 2s, D7653 and D7654. Note that the train is slightly longer than the one hauled by the Brush, hence the extra motive power, although of course the Sulzer Type 2 was rated at 1250 horsepower against the 147? h.p. of the Brush locomotives. These particular Sulzers' (BP works Nos.8063 and 8064) were to be amongst the last locomotives built by the famous Manchester company which, for a century or so, was responsible for supplying the world's railways with more than 800? locomotives of all types including many of the Garratt articulated steam locomotives. During the weeks following this event, Toton depot would take delivery of the last ever Beyer, Peacock built product when Type 2 D7659 was released to traffic. Both of the Bo-Bos pictured here were renumbered under the TOPS scheme and became Class 25 Nos.303 and 304. Uncanny, perhaps, but note that the last digit of their respective first and second British Railways numbers and their maker's numbers – 8063 and 8064 – were the same! Since their withdrawal in the eighties, at least five of the Beyer, Peacock built Sulzers' have been preserved including, and most appropriately indeed, D7659 itself. Neither of these two were lucky though, D7653 ended up on the scrap mountain in the Vic Berry yard at Leicester whilst D7654 was broken up at BR Swindon! *D.H.Beecroft.*

After the Type 2s had vacated the section, Brush Type 4 D1819 appeared from the south with this long train of mineral empties headed y four brake vans of varying styles and liveries. Bound for Kirkby-in-Ashfield, the Co-Co's real work would start after leaving the main ne at Pye Bridge. One of the Brush-built 47s, D1819 was released to traffic in February 1965 and was allocated to Toton (actually the ewly created Nottingham Division – D16). From this angle it is possible to see the outline of the erstwhile station platforms and the oundations of the Up side waiting room. The necessary dog-leg of the freight lines, caused by the station's presence, is also apparent. or those interested in the brake vans, the following details have been come to light: 1st van – Standard BR 20-ton fitted or through-piped an, with concrete ballast slabs; 2nd van – is similar but unfitted; 3rd van – is also fitted or through-piped, but has shorter side steps and no oncrete slabs, indicating a vehicle of LNER origin; 4th van – appears to be a Southern Railway 4-wheel brake van, with horizontal planking n the end partitions, two steps fixed to the lower edge of the deep solebar and one (short) long step with three brackets! *D.H.Beecroft.* 5

Looking north at Shipley Gate as a BR Sulzer Type 2 D5185 rushes past with a returning Saturday only (SO) holiday train in June 1966. Up until the first year of Nationalisation there used to be a passenger station known as Shipley Gate at this place but which closed for business on Friday 27ᵗʰ August 1948. Opened by the Midland Railway in 1851, when the main line consisted just two tracks, the station eventually had a near neighbour – though separated by a canal, a river and another canal – when the Great Northern opened their own station at the east end of the half mile lane connecting the two stations in August 1876. With a duplication of facilities the newly formed British Railways was quick to close the ex-MR station because the former GNR establishment with the long-winded title of Newthorpe & Greasley was nearer to the southern edge of the habitation of Eastwood with its 6,000 or so residents. The latter station existed until 7 January 1963 when it became a casualty of the Beeching cuts and it too was closed although the last train to use the place was the final working from Pinxton hauled by B1 No.61299 on the evening of Saturday 5ᵗʰ January. Note that our train here is made up almost entirely of former LMS stock, Stanier 'Period 3' I'm reliably informed, except vehicle seven (BR Mk1 SK) and possibly vehicle 8 also BR Mk1. The LMS stock was by now nearing the end of its life and would normally spend all week stuck in a siding to be used only at weekends in the summer months. Winter usage might entail the odd football excursion but otherwise the carriages would be redundant for much of the year. The Type 2 diesel electric locomotive, another of the Toton allocation, was one of the Darlington built batch which was just three years old. It became Class 25 No.035 and would go on to be preserved after withdrawal in March 1987. *D.H.Beecroft.*

Just a mile or so north of Toton is Stanton Gate where a large group of sidings associated with the local industry were located on the Up side of the line. In this view of 'Peak' D110, heading north with an oil train on a summer evening in July 1969, we can glimpse some of those sidings on the left. This was a busy place, a funnel perhaps, a sort of 'coming together' with the main line from the north, the numerous branches feeding in coal trains and traffic from rail connected industrial concerns. Then of course you had the northbound traffic such as this! It's nearly all gone now: sidings, industry, collieries, much of the traffic, and the signals. Note the parachute water tank which was certainly a redundant piece of furniture, even then in '69. What about D110? Another of the Crewe-builds, dating from July 1961, it became 45065 in January 1975 and remained on the Toton strength until withdrawn ten years later. Vic Berry purchased it from BR and it was cut up in July 1988. *D.H.Beecroft.*

D8180 and D8164 with an iron ore train at Stanton Junction, Thursday 23rd May 1968. Working from Colwick yard and bound for the ironworks at Stanton, the train would have reached this location via Weekday Cross, Nottingham Victoria (closed and demolished by now but two running lines existed on the east side of the former station site), Bagthorpe junction, Basford North, Kimberley, Awsworth and Ilkeston. Until recent years the iron ore for Stanton works had originated from quarries near Belvoir, at Denton and had been a regular traffic over the GNR since the 1890s; latterly though imported ore had become the staple for the furnaces at the ironworks. The Type 1s were just entering the two and a half mile-long branch for Stanton having picked up the single line token from the signalman. Our intrepid photographer is standing on what had previously been the Great Northern main line from Nottingham to Derby (Frairgate) but the chances of a train running him down were minimal as the line was all but closed. *David Dalton.*

Having delivered the 'fulls' and picked up the empties from the Stanton works , a Sulzer Type 2 and EE Type 1 combination stop at Stanton Junction box to hand back the token to the waiting signalman. Identifiable in this 23rd May 1968 view is a weathered Type 2 D7537 belonging to the D15 - Leicester Division at that time. The Type 1 was probably from D16 - Nottingham Division (Toton) as none of the class were allocated to D15; so how the combination came about is of interest. This was the second to last day of these iron ore workings traversing the former GNR route and on the following Monday, 27th, the line from here to the southern end of Victoria station was closed; in effect it was closed from Saturday 25th, there being no Sunday working. Apparently the last train was headed by EE Type 1 D8016 and another unidentified member of the same class. The signal box is worth a mention in that it was GN Type 2 box built to a variation of the design used for the Great Eastern/GNR Joint line in Lincolnshire and was provided with a Saxby & Farmer locking frame with 66 levers. It was unusual in having a separate lavatory block situated behind and apart from the box rather than on the landing. From this position we are looking east towards Ilkeston with the broad sweep of Manners Road bridge giving the impression of spanning a large number of railway tracks which it in fact did with a number of sidings paralleling the running tracks between this point and the substantial station at Ilkeston. Branching off to the left is the track bed of the erstwhile Heanor branch which closed in 1964. That branch had served a number of collieries along its route and was one of the reasons the Great Northern spent so much money penetrating so far west from Grantham. *David Dalton.*

NOTTINGHAM & ITS SUBURBS

Travelling along the former Midland Railway's Leen valley line, Toton based Brush Type 4 D1829 keeps a tight reign on this heavy coal train as it travels south through Basford Vernon in July 1966. The train – 8F79 – is loaded with power station coal and originated from one of the seven collieries situated between this Nottingham suburb and Annesley at the head of the valley. Barely sixteen months old, the Co-Co is hardly looking its best and beneath all that grime is a two-tone green livery. Note that certain details of the locomotive are clean or at least 'picked out' – the yellow warning panel across the front, the fleet number, the electrification warning flashes, and the BR crest. Toton had a large fleet of these 2750 horsepower locomotives allocated during this period when 'pits' in this sector of the Nottinghamshire coalfield were at their busiest producing in excess of nine million tons of saleable coal a year. Besides local customers, the Nottingham Division of British Railways provided for the transport of coal to utilities and industrial concerns in the southern counties of England too; cement producers in Kent, and the base load power station at Didcot, were two such customers requiring vast quantities of coal on a daily basis. However, the latter utility went straight to the MGR delivery system when commissioned, these ancient hoppers having no place in that new facility. The more likely destination for this train is probably Castle Donington power station or those at Drakelow, Staythorpe or Willington. The road to the right of the Bulwell sandstone-built boundary wall is Vernon Road on which most of the building illustrated, still exist albeit with modernised windows and some shops converted into residences. The buildings with the large chimney consisted of one of the many dye works in this textile city. By July 1966 trolleybus operations on Nottingham City Transport's services 43 and 44, along Vernon Road, had ceased and the big six-wheel Brush vehicles replaced by Daimler Fleetlines, Leyland Atlanteans and AEC Renowns. *D.H.Beecroft.*

Super power for the Up *THAMES-CLYDE EXPRESS* in July 1969 as 'Peaks' 44 and 111 prepare to depart from platform 4 at Nottingham Midland station. Note that the bridge which once carried the erstwhile Great Central Railway over the Midland station still dominates the scene. It was to be 1978 before it was finally dismantled. However, forty-odd year on and the southern extension to the Nottingham tramway system (*NET* – Nottingham Express Transit) is soon to follow the same course of the old railway and a new bridge will be required for that! The station in 1969 and even today is little changed from its opening by the Midland, but changes are afoot as a multi-storey car park is being built and major alterations are planned to take place in 2013, although many of the buildings will remain largely unaltered – perhaps a little generous given that the station was compared to a 'Victorian Gents Toilet' some years ago! *D.H.Beecroft.*

A St Pancras-Sheffield service with D123 at the head, stands at platform 3, ready for the 'off' from Nottingham Midland in Januar 1974. Renumbering of the BR locomotive fleet under the TOPS scheme was underway by now and D123 would become 45125 durin the following April – miraculously the big diesel still sports its 'D' prefix some five years after they were abolished. The GC bridge is stil casting its huge shadow over the proceedings beneath. *D.H.Beecroft.*

Whereas in steam days it was possible to run a passenger train from St Pancras to Leeds (City), calling on the way at Nottingham (Midland), with the same locomotives at the head and with no reversing required, the same could not be said in 1974. Closure of the alternative route to London via Melton Mowbray meant certain Midland line expresses headed for destinations north of Sheffield but calling at Nottingham had to work into the city from Trent, have a change of locomotive, and direction, and retrace their tracks as far as Lenton junction where the line to Trowell junction put them back on a south-north heading along the Erewash. Ex-works 45020 (D26) has just taken over from 45123 (D52) THE LANCASHIRE FUSILIER with a St Pancras express, made up of Mk.2A stock, at platform 3 in September 1974. *D.H.Beecroft.* 13

Yet another Type 2, our old friend D5185 shows off its mixed traffic capability now as it gingerly descends the bank from Bagthorp
Junction with an interesting goods working consisting of dozens of military vehicles on flat wagons - no doubt M-o-D owned Warflats an
Warwells? The date was 23rd May 1968 a time when the United Kingdom was not involved in any major or even minor military conflicts
Therefore, the movement of large amounts of military 'kit' by rail was either to move a unit to a training area with rail facilities (such
facilities were rare even in those days) or to transport redundant 'kit' to a storage facility which did have rail access (quite a number existe
in England in that Cold War period, especially around the counties of Derbyshire and Nottinghamshire). The appearance of Morri
2-tonners, and Austin K2 ambulances, points to a time when such vehicles were being 'stored' by the Army. So, although the origin o
this special working – 8T39 – is unknown, the destination was possibly M-o-D Ruddington which had a connection to the ex GC route fo
some years after this working took place. MoD Bicester has also been suggested. Perhaps someone with local knowledge would know o
the working and can enlighten us all with some certainty. Note that the train is not working out of the 'Rat Hole' or even wrong-line fron
Basford North. The locomotive and half of its train is approaching 'right line' after working along the GC route 'wrong-line' on the Dow
as far as the junction signal box where it has crossed to the Up line. With some certainty we can mention that the days of the GC rout
are numbered – in single figures by now – with closure of this stretch taking place on 26th May 1968. No trace of a railway now exists her
the cutting having been re-filled to approximately its original contour and houses built on top. The high embankment which once carrie
Bagthorpe junction has also been removed and the area developed with housing. *David Dalton.*

n July 1966 one of Tinsley's recently acquired Brush Type 4s, Crewe-built D1572, climbs the bank of the old GCR route at New Basford fter its stop at Nottingham (Victoria) with train 1N83. The Poole to Bradford (Saturdays Only, I do believe) was, as can be seen, made p of Southern Region green stock. Although more than two years old on this date, the Co-Co looks rather clean and may well have had a isit to main works to get that kind of finish to its bodywork. Becoming 47018 in March 1974, the '47' had been allocated in the meantime Holbeck, Gateshead and Healey Mills prior to a settled allocation to Stratford in January 1972. During the next twenty-two years it was ariously attached to depots at Gateshead (again), Eastfield, Crewe, and Tinsley. Aged thirty years, 47018 was withdrawn in March 1994 nd then sold for scrap to Cooper's Metals, Sheffield. The New Basford carriage sheds on the Up side of the line, had a diesel multiple nit fuelling and servicing facility provided by the Eastern Region. However, shortly after completion the ex GCR route and everything R in Nottingham went over to the Dark Side (as somebody recently put it!) when it was taken over by the LMR. Apparently the facility emained unused to the very end. In 2011 almost nothing of the railway illustrated here remains. *D.H.Beecroft.*

15

Further down the incline, towards Nottingham's Victoria station, on another summer Saturday in 1966, an English Electric Type 3, D6743 emerges from Sherwood Rise tunnel with that Poole-Bradford train in tow. This time the express was made up of Eastern Region stock including a Gresley open at the front of the formation. Tinsley had supplied the motive power on this day and the Type 3 must have relished the chance to stretch its legs after its normal labours moving freight around the Sheffield district. The EE Type 3 was perhaps *the* success story of all the early diesel types purchased by BR under the Modernisation Plan. The first examples were put into traffic in December 1960 with a total of 309 being put to work during the following five years. D6743 was one of the examples built at Vulcan Foundry - just over twenty percent of the total were erected at the Robert Stephenson & Hawthorn plant in Darlington - and went new to Darnall shed in June 1962. Extremely reliable, and versatile, this locomotive type outlived its contemporaries by decades and became one of the longest lived classes in BR diesel history albeit with a certain amount of rebuilding and updating to some members to reinforce that claim. Renumbered to 37043 in February 1974 (that seems to have been an extremely busy month for the painters and transfer applicators at the depots), our subject became 37354 in June 1988 when it was given an Intermediate level overhaul (apparently full refurbishment was financially out of the question) and equipped with re-geared but salvaged CP7 bogies from condemned Class 50s (similar bogies from the Deltics were also used on other members of the class involved in this scheme). Reverting to 37043 in June 1992, the '37' was finally condemned in January 2000 and cut up in May 2003 at Simms Metals in Beeston, which is only a few miles west of this location. During its operational years, D6743 (37043) migrated to March depot after Tinsley, then on to Stratford before moving to Glasgow Eastfield (where it carried the name LOCH LOMOND from October 1981 to June 1986). The cutting here is now a housing estate with partial fill and children's play area up to the tunnel mouth, only about 3-4ft of the top of the arch being visible, and barred. *David Dalton.*

This brand-new pair of BR 350 h.p. 0-6-0 diesel shunters, 13247 and 13246, arrived at Nottingham shed in May 1956; the illustration here is actually depicting their early afternoon arrival on shed from Derby works. Four other Derby-built shunters had preceded them during the previous winter – 13083 to 13086 – and now it was time to expand the fleet at 16A. However, only one more new example arrived – 13290, also from Derby, in December 1956. Our two here were renumbered D3247 (March 1961) and D3246 (December 1960) respectively. All of these particular locomotives became Class 08 under the TOPS scheme but mention must be made of the earlier Derby built 0-6-0 diesel shunters which became Class 11 (although none took up that classification and were withdrawn before they could do so) six of which came new to Nottingham starting with No.12097 in December 1951, followed by 12098 to 12102 during the early months of 1952. That class was recognised as the true forerunner of the BR Standard 0-6-0DE shunter - Class 08. These two were delivered in green livery and, if you let your imagination focus, you can still smell that 'newness' which accompanied every diesel locomotive at delivery. *David Dalton.* 17

Some drastic changes had occurred to the railway system around the East Midlands from the end of steam traction to mid-1974. This is the western throat of Nottingham Midland, or simply Nottingham under British Rail, where track rationalisation has taken place reducing the number of tracks drastically by nearly a half from what was available ten years previously. Class 31 252 has just emerged from the station precincts with an empty ballast train, consisting a pair of BR 40-ton Walrus bogie hoppers and three BR 24-ton Dogfish wagons, on a Sunday in September 1974, judging by the amount of road traffic on Carrington Street. Unlike some station frontages, and indeed the stations themselves, the 1904 facade of the Midland station survived the aforementioned rationalisation – and the insults – and lives on in the 21st Century, fronting a station which is as busy as ever. The white painted wooden gables of the former MR goods depot were soon to become another casualty of cuts as much of the railway infrastructure on either side of the main line as far west as Lenton junction was pulled down and the vacant land sold off. The gables are now replaced by the gables of the Magistrates and County Court building (the railway history of the site actually goes back to 1839 as the location of the original Midland Counties terminus). The vacant land on this (south) side of the '31' used to carry the Goods lines which enabled freight traffic to avoid passing through the passenger station, unlike now when a long tank train heading to or from the Immingham area can bring the entire station to a stop. Not good when there is nominally a timetabled movement every three minutes in or out of the station! This area is now the railway staff car park. *D.H.Beecroft.*

Another coal train from the Leen valley collieries, this one powered by 'Peak' No.50 THE KING'S SHROPSHIRE LIGHT INFANTRY, passes through the derelict station at Radford in September 1970 with power station coal. D50, to revert back to its original fleet number, was one of the 1962 Crewe-built batch of 'Peaks' and was put into traffic in May of that year, initially allocated to Derby. Of course, with the eventual concentration of all the East Midlands motive power to one site, the 'Peak' ended up at Toton where duties such as this awaited it. Such was the versatility of this class (TOPS Class 45 by now), the following day this particular locomotive might have been powering an express from Nottingham to St Pancras or to Leeds and beyond but today its time for a slog doing what the railways were invented for. Not knowing the actual working, there is every reason to believe that No.50 was en route with its train to Toton yard where marshalling would get this load ready to its intended destination. This location was no stranger to coal workings from the Leen valley and for more than a century literally millions of tons have passed this place hauled by numerous types of 0-6-0 steam locomotives; 2-8-0s were latterly in charge of such workings. However, in the age of the diesel anything can turn-up, as we have already seen. What of the station's history? Opened for passengers in September 1876, the station had replaced another which had opened in 1848 but which had to be re-sited when the junction for the Trowell line was constructed. Closure of this second station had occurred only recently, in October 1964. Ilkeston Road (A609) crosses over the railway on the bridge where the overhead catenary, and wires, once used by the defunct Nottingham City Transport three-axle Brush-built trolleybuses of service No.39 were by now in use for street lighting. Beyond the bridge, just out of shot to the right, are Player's bonded warehouses. Here, even in the 1960s, a cheque to HM Customs & Excise for £1 million was signed every morning to release the tobacco for the day's manufacturing! 'Peak' No.50 became 45040 in January 1975. In July 1987, whilst allocated to Tinsley, it was withdrawn but later took up Departmental employment. *D.H.Beecroft.*

In August 1969 a pair of unidentified English Electric Type 1s head, light engine, along the Down slow towards Nottingham as an express, with 'Peak' D86 in charge, leaves the city. The location is Lenton South junction where much of the Leen valley coal traffic joins the east-west main line en route to Toton or other destinations via Trent. Steam has been banished from BR metals for just a year and many railway enthusiasts have 'thrown in the towel' with the diesel fleet. However, for those enthusiasts who stuck with the railway scene post-steam, the East Midlands became the place to visit. Not only did Toton depot offer a feast of locomotives at weekends but some of its outstation stabling points could offer up numerous units too. During this period of East Midlands railway history, places such as Colwick, Westhouses, Kirkby-in-Ashfield, Burton, Coalville and Nottingham conjured up a hundred or more resting locomotives between them. Of course in 1969 there was still diversity amongst the BR fleet allocated to and visiting the area: 08, 20, 24, 25, 31, 37, 40, 44, 45, 46, and 47. HSTs were a thing of the future and the fleet of diesel multiple units plying the rails in 1969 still included much of the Modernisation Plan stock which were many in number and certainly varied. Of course changes were taking place continually on BR and although the Beeching purges were just about finished, another load of closures were creeping up as BR sought to rid itself of its huge deficit and modernise what was worth keeping, not to mention selling off vast tracts of the land which it had inherited. The locomotives illustrated represented classes which were, for all intents and purposes, successful and therefore had some years of service left in them: D86 for instance, which was already eight years old, would work until 1987, as 45105, before being condemned. As a class, the '20s' would not only work for an eternity but many of them would then be exported to mainland Europe for another stint of hard work! Of course all that was in the future and here is illustrated the old order as it existed in 1969. The line in the immediate foreground, off to the right, leads to Clifton Colliery and Wilford power station. The line on which the two 21-ton, double-door, mineral wagons are standing, and the adjacent line, led to Nottingham Royal Ordnance Factory – pit, power station and ROF are now all gone. Nottingham Castle (not the original but a 17th Century ducal mansion on that site) stands on Castle Rock. To the left of that you might be able to see the dome of 'Little John' (the name of the bell, as in 'Big Ben'), of the Council House in the Old Market Square. *D.H.Beecroft.*

Lenton South junction, June 1974. 'Peak' 45103 heads out of town on the Up fast with a St Pancras bound express. Five years on from the previous view a certain amount of rationalisation and modernisation has taken place with the signalling being the most obvious although by now it was under the control of Trent power box. The London expresses are still in the hands of the 'Peaks' although they had nearly all been renumbered under the TOPS scheme by this date. 45103, formerly D117, still had another thirteen years work ahead of it. The train consists: BR Mk1 SK and BSK leading, with the remainder, except for the catering vehicle, Mk2As. The track to the erstwhile Clifton Colliery and Wilford power station is now lifted but the track bed is still evident. The large factory complex above the train was the ROF which has now gone to be replaced with a retail and business park. *D.H.Beecroft.*

21

This next view, also in June 1974, is taken a little to the west of the previous illustration, with the camera now also facing west as 45011 brings an express from St Pancras into Nottingham on the Down fast beneath the Nottingham Ring Road bridge (then A614, now A52). It was here, on Thursday 16th December 1971, that a morning parcels train from Liverpool to Nottingham, and a coal train from Bestwood Colliery to Derby were in head-on collision. Two drivers and a guard were killed in the incident which occurred when the parcels train approaching on the Down fast line ran into the coal train. The junction, a so-called 'ladder' crossing, required that Up trains from the branch had to travel some distance along the Down fast before crossing over to the Up fast. Although the crossing is obscured by the train here, it was located about where the second and third coaches are positioned. The two Class 20s on the coal train, 8115 and 8142 were both badly damaged but the Class 25 heading the parcels train, Toton based 7605, was so badly damaged that it was condemned immediately and broken up at Derby works shortly afterwards. Judging by the exhaust put out by 45011, the locomotive is still under power, possibly having stopped at Beeston. The signals at the rear of the train are fitted with 'feathers' which are just discernible and are there to indicate direction changes. The signal above the goods line has one such 'feather' whilst that over the main has two, indicating a move to the goods line and/or a move around the corner to Lenton North. *D.H.Beecroft.*

In the days when green was still the dominant livery for BR diesel locomotives and the 'D' prefix was still prevalent, a previous acquaintance, 'Peak' D50, heads north after negotiating Lenton North junction and the Beeston canal bridge in April 1969. Note that the driver is glancing back to make sure his train has cleared the spur. Except for a handful of vans, much of the train – 8T30 – is made up of 16-ton mineral wagons loaded with coal; where on earth could that lot be headed? This is a Class 8 (unfitted) freight with the four BR 12-ton ventilated vans included to provide a fitted head – assuming the hoses are connected. The first three vans seem to be plywood-sided. Vans 1 and 4 have corrugated ends and single vent hoods at each end whilst 2 and 3 would appear to be built to Dia.1/205, a GWR design with two vent hoods at each end. Van 4 has sliding doors and was probably built to an LMS design, Dia.1/200; the other vans had cupboard doors. Nowadays, the area is still recognisable, the large electricity pylon in place along with the houses albeit some modernised and extended. There are no freights though, just DMUs providing a half-hourly service on the Robin Hood line and hourly Leeds and Liverpool services via Radford junction and the branch to Trowell. *D.H.Beecroft.*

With the massive cooling towers of Ratcliffe-on-Trent power station dominating the background, 45115 speeds south along the Up fast at Kegworth with a St Pancras express in September 1974. For more than twenty years the Sulzer Type 4 (Class 45) was the mainstay motive power of the Midland Lines express passenger working and most of them were allocated to Toton for maintenance. It was not until the advent of the High Speed Train on the route out of St Pancras that these magnificent machines could slow down from their continuou sprints. It would be interesting to know what kind of mileage's these locomotives actually completed during their lifetimes. Towards the end of their lives, while allocated to Tinsley depot, the '45s' could still turn up on occasional London services and put in good performances 45141 (by then unofficially named ZEPHYR) ran for a good few miles at near on 100 m.p.h. (self timed) whilst working one such London service. Our subject here also ended up at Tinsley and, was given the unofficial name APOLLO prior to withdrawal in May 1988. After long period in store at the virtually disused marshalling yard it was hauled away to MC Metals in Glasgow for breaking up. *D.H.Beecroft.*

Amongst the many 'strange decisions' taken by BR under the auspices of the 1955 Modernisation Plan was the initial allocation of thirty-six 1250 h.p. Type 2 Bo-Bo locomotives built by the Birmingham Railway Carriage & Wagon Company, to the Midland Lines of the LMR in 1962. That particular batch went initially to Cricklewood where they were employed on suburban services from St Pancras, along with empty stock duties and cross-London freight workings. Besides the LMR allocation, ten had been sent to Thornaby in North-Eastern Region whilst twenty-two had gone to the Scottish Region at Eastfield. Externally they were virtually identical to the earlier 1160 h.p. Type 2s produced by the same maker in 1958/59 except that these later locomotives had four-character head code boxes fitted. In 1963 some of the London based engines moved to the Derby and Nottingham areas and places such as Burton-on-Trent shed started crew training on this type. Maintaining an old Derby tradition, the Midland Line engines came under Derby works for heavy maintenance so light engine workings to and from Derby brought the Cricklewood machines to the East Midlands on occasion. However, by August 1968, when a filthy D5384 and a respectable looking D5410 were caught on camera, heading south along the Midland main line, a number of the class had migrated to both the Leicester Division and the Nottingham Division (that is the old 15 and 16 shed areas of the steam era). The pair, both still attached to Cricklewood's allocation, were passing the site of the erstwhile passenger station at Hathern, after a visit to the shops. Note that the station here, opened in conjunction with the Midland's independent route into London in 1868, was closed in January 1960. *D.H.Beecroft.*

25

Two years earlier, in June 1966, another grotty looking Type 2, Derby-built Sulzer D7575 of November 1963, brings a local passenger train from Leicester to Nottingham, past the derelict station at Hathern. Renumbered 25225 in February 1974, the Bo-Bo was by then resident on the Western Region at Laira. Compared with most, this '25' had an early demise being condemned at Laira in October 1980 and then being cut up at Swindon the following month. Now, the station might be derelict but the architecture was still sound – just look at that chimney stack! Nowadays the station is in private use and looks reasonably well cared for. At one time Hathern was the boundary between the Trent and Leicester power signalling areas. *D.H.Beecroft.*

A Sunday diversion brings unusual traffic to the freight-only line through Pinxton in March 1975. The normal fare for this line is coal trains, coal trains and more coal trains. The landscape in the area was constantly changing due to the presence of the collieries and their ever changing spoil heaps. The line is steeply graded and tight bends abound resulting in a 20 m.p.h. speed limit from Kirkby to Pye Bridge. Loose coupled coal trains were still banked from Pye Bridge and along this stretch, even in diesel days. However on this rather pleasant weekend the passengers on the diverted Newcastle-Bristol express have been treated to a nice little tour through a section of the Nottinghamshire coalfield, and on the way travelling on some 'freight only' trackage over which many railway enthusiasts would have paid a small fortune to traverse. The motive power is Gateshead based 46046 (ex D183) which is nicely turned out whilst the train is made up entirely of BR Mark 1 stock – obviously the cross-country services had yet to be upgraded to Mk.2 carriages. The consist would have diverged from its usual route near Sheffield, taking a left at Foxlow junction, through Seymour yard, on to Elmton & Cresswell junction then south through Nether Langwith, Shirebrook, Mansfield, Kirkby-in-Ashfield, then Pinxton prior to joining the Erewash valley main line at Pye Bridge junction, just a couple of miles from this location. More than a dozen deep mines would have been passed during the diversion but it's probable that none of the passengers would have noticed anyway. A similar journey today, if it were possible in its entirety, would reveal half a dozen new passenger stations on the Robin Hood line but not one working colliery. *D.H.Beecroft.*

27

Immaculate Brush Type 4 D1634 stands alongside the former platform 1 at the closed Mansfield (Town) station on a sunny Easter Monday afternoon – 19th April 1965 – having just run round its train. From this position D1634 hauled the consist across to the Up line and then reversed and propelled the train into platform 2, nearest the camera. The Co-Co had worked into the town with a Carlisle United football club supporters special (1X75) from that most northerly of English cities, and is ready to work back home retracing the route taken to get here from the WCML. The game, against Mansfield Town at Field Mill, was a Division 3 fixture which the home side won 2-0. As was the trait of some football fans at that time, trouble broke out in the town centre between the rival factions after the match but the train, unlike others during this period of the Sixties', luckily remained unscathed. Now then, just look at the Type 4 which by now was nearly six months old! Its condition was due to the fact that many of the staff at Upperby motive power depot were CU fans and they apparently cleaned all the locomotives designated for CUFC football special haulage, carrying on a traditional going back a number of years. When D1634 was put into traffic during the previous November, it was allocated to Crewe but it eventually ended up at Toton depot where many others from the same Crewe-built batch had gone initially. Note the remnants of the steam age cluttering up the opposite platform end. A final word about the football element – a return fixture took place at Carlisle the following day but this time the Stags came unstuck losing three nil to Carlisle who were apparently the Division leaders. *David Dalton.*

BR Sulzer Type 4 D146, with brake tender attached, powers a Birmingham-bound coal train through Repton & Willington station in June 1966. At the time, the Type 4 was allocated to the Midland Lines pool but would have attended Toton for maintenance. Before the end of the decade D146 will have been transferred to the Western Region, first to Bristol and then Plymouth, with visits to Toton being extremely rare until Gateshead acquired its services. Becoming 46009, the 1-Co-Co-1 was withdrawn in October 1983 and taken into Departmental stock as 97401*. This mineral train may well have been collected from Toton Up yard but sometimes block loads from a specific colliery and bound for certain customers, were worked direct to destination without being processed at Toton Up yard. In the background can be seen the chimneys and cooling towers of the two Willington power stations – the 392 megawatt 'A' station opened in 1959, whilst the 376 megawatt 'B' station opened in 1963. Both utilities would be long-term customers for rail-borne coal. The railway station here opened in August 1839 and was originally called Willington, changing to Willington & Repton before finally becoming Repton & Willington. Closed in March 1968 as part of the Beeching cuts, the station re-opened for passengers in May 1995, using the original 1839 title – just Willington! The name boards used for the re-opening of Willington station were embellished with the Ivanhoe Line crest. It was planned, at the time, to re-open the line through Coalville and Ashby-De-la-Zouch to passenger traffic, thus creating a circular route from Derby via Long Eaton (Sawley) through Loughborough and the re-opened stations at Barrow-on-Soar, Sileby and Syston to Leicester. Then, onwards from Leicester, through Ashby and Coalville to Burton-on-Trent, finally returning to Derby through Willington. The name boards at Barrow, Sileby and Syston also had the Ivanhoe Line crest but unfortunately the line linking them never got past the planning stages due to lack of finance. There are attempts to resurrect the scheme so that one day a class 158 may actually reach Ashby-De-la-Zouch as the destination has been programmed into the electronic display on those units since they were built. *D.H.Beecroft.*

46009 became famous overnight as the locomotive used to prove the supposed invulnerability of the rail-borne flasks carrying nuclear waste. During the test, in July 1984, the driverless 'Peak' was allowed to collide with a flask at a speed near to 100 m.p.h. Thankfully, the flask remained unscathed, much to everybody's relief, but the '46' was completely wrecked and was cut up at the test site shortly afterwards.

Barton & Walton is situated further south from Willington on the old Midland line from Derby to Birmingham and in June 1966 most of the freight traffic was still in the hands of Stanier 8F 2-8-0s and BR Standard 9Fs. Such was the case on Wednesday 22nd until an English Electric Type 4, D219 CARONIA, came thumping along from the Burton direction with a loaded westbound coal train. It wasn't unusual to see Type 4s working goods traffic on this stretch of the line during that period in time but to have one of the Western Lines fleet employed on such duties was quite rare. Just where the train had originated and its eventual destination are unknown but at least we have a photographic record of the event. Of course, by now the West Coast main line electrification was proceeding towards its completion and most of the WCML based Type 4s had lost their express passenger train status to the growing fleet of electric locomotives – they had in effect been 'cascaded' down to the level of working freights, even on *other* railways! The station here had closed in August 1958, just a year before this 1-Co-Co-1 was put into traffic. However, the station's origins go back to the earliest period of the railways with the first one being opened by the Birmingham & Derby Junction Railway in August 1839. That establishment was replaced in 1871 by the Midland Railway when an overbridge (situated at the south end of the platforms) replaced the original level crossing. The remains of the building shown on the Down platform in this illustration was once a rather ornate waiting room, albeit roofless now, with the main station building behind the photographer. *D.H.Beecroft.*

The more usual motive power passing through Barton & Walton on express passenger services was of course the BR Sulzer Type 4s – the 'Peaks' – and shortly after the passage of the '40' on that Wednesday in June 1966, a '46' in the shape of D143 rushed through the derelict station with a Newcastle-Bristol working made up of maroon livery BR Mk.1 stock. As built, this batch of 'Peaks' numbered from D138 to D193 and were all fitted with Brush electrical equipment; those from D11 to D137 had Crompton Parkinson electrical equipment and were eventually classified '45' under the TOPS scheme. All the 'Peaks' had Sulzer prime movers with the first ten (D1-D10) having 2300 h.p. examples whilst the rest had 2500 h.p. engines. They were impressive locomotives and were much quieter, especially when accelerating and at speed, than their English Electric counterparts, the '40s' – the 'Peaks' could indeed creep up, even at 80 m.p.h.! Appearing ex-works with some recently acquired road dirt, D143 became 46006 in February 1974 (unlike the '45s', all of Class 46 were numbered in an orderly fashion in the order of building so that D138 became 46001 and D193 became 46056, although why the class terminated at D193 is still a mystery to this compiler). It is worth recalling that on the Midland Railway, prior to Grouping, Derby was the 'centre of the universe' therefore all lines leading to Derby were Up whilst those leading away were Down; things remained pretty much the same after 1923. A number of Midland Railway features show up in this view; the diagonal planked fencing and, some distance from the camera, the double post telegraph pole. *D.H.Beecroft.*

31

Applying the brakes for the stop at Leicester, 'Peak' D78 passes Leicester North signal box in March 1969 with an afternoon St Pancras bound express. In the background the former steam motive power depot is still very much intact, the coaling and ash plants standing proud though never to be used again; the threat of demolition was not far away for those structures. The roundhouse is now empty and idle, the few diesels which grace the depot now stabling in the yard or entering the service shed in the right background. A letter in the July 1964 edition of *Modern Railways* went on at length about BR diesel locomotive policy and its problems', in particular the correspondent asked what was to be made of the dieselisation of the Midland Division of the LMR and the apparent difficulties in keeping discipline amongst the staff at Cricklewood diesel depot. Because of the latter problem, the rapidly growing diesel locomotive fleet based at the southern end of the Midland main line was being maintained at Leicester depot where, in common with other Midland Division depots, there was virtually no equipment or staff to deal with diesel locomotives at the present time. *signed "Dip. Sam"*. Of course, Leicester diesel depot lasted well into the privatisation era, being latterly used by EWS but was then abandoned. However, the servicing shed is still intact with fuel roads in front. Recently the weeds have been cleared indicating, perhaps, future re-use. Note the semaphores which were replaced by colour lights and a new Leicester power box in the 1980s; the latter has itself become obsolete and was scheduled to close with the signalling taken over by the East Midlands Integrated Control Centre at Derby in Christmas 2011. *D.H.Beecroft.*

DERBY WORKS

Derby, circa 1965! This depressing sight of condemned and rotting diesel locomotives at the former LMS workshops was a regular occurrence in the Sixties. Derby could well claim to be the birthplace of British diesel locomotive building and repair because it was here in 1931 that the first attempt by the LMS to construct a diesel shunting locomotive took place. Admitted, steam technology was never far away and the frames of the 0-6-0 diesel-hydraulic – numbered 1831 – were salvaged from an 0-6-0T to which a diesel engine and hydraulic 'gearing' was fitted. It was to be 1934 before that particular one-off was taken into LMS stock and it was put to work at Derby where it was to prove to the LMS authorities that diesel traction was useful; initially expensive but cheaper, in the long run, than steam locomotives! Between the rebuilding of 0-6-0T No.1831 and 1939, a number of contractor built diesel shunters were purchased by the LMS and during the May of 1939, Derby began turning out its first true diesel-electric shunting locomotives in the shape of the jackshaft drive 0-6-0s Nos.7080 to 7082. More of course were to follow but WW2 held back development of a main line diesel locomotive until the very eve of Nationalisation when LMS 10000 was introduced to the world in December 1947. Sister 10001 followed in July 1948 and the two then settled down to a myriad of tests, earning a living, and attending various exhibitions. By December 1962 No.10000 had finished its work (10001 as not condemned until March 1966) and was set to languish in the works yard at Derby until condemned the following year. However, it was to be a resident at this place for a further four years before it was towed away for scrapping at a private breakers yard. British Railways, with the attitude prevailing at that time, would not even consider the preservation of the pioneer main line diesel locomotive – Co-Co 10000. Here is that same locomotive sharing the scrap line with two of the Southern Region built 1-Co-Co-1 diesel-electrics 10203 and 10202, both incidentally withdrawn at the same time as 10000. The SR locomotives, along with the third member of that trio 10201, ended up in the same scrap yard as 10000 – 'Honest John' Cashmore's at Great Bridge. Following the success of the replica A1, TORNADO, and the rapidly progressing Baby Deltic replica at Barrow Hill depot, there are moves afoot to build a replica 10000!! *David Dalton.*

33

Smell that paint! BR Sulzer Type 2 D5010 has its first outing in the works yard at Derby in March 1959. More than new, the Bo-Bo has yet to receive the fuel to run its engines but once that has been done the 1160 h.p. diesel will have been tested at the works prior to undertaking road tests which usually involved a trip out to Cheadle Heath and back with some passenger stock. If all went well, and it usually did, the new diesel would be sent to its designated depot which, in the case of D5010, was Crewe South shed. The first twenty of this class – D5000 to D5019 – were all allocated to Crewe South when new but most of that first batch soon transferred to the Southern Region at Hither Green depot, our subject here being amongst them. By the summer of 1962 many had returned to the LMR, D5010 taking up residence at Rugby. In later years those fairings along the solebars would be removed (or left off!).Having perhaps a chequered if not interesting career, D5010 ended up at Eastfield depot where it was withdrawn in October 1975. It had been withdrawn initially in January 1969 but not apparently re-instated until September 1975! Renumbering to 24010 was carried out during April 1974, whilst in store!

Before Derby starting building main-line diesel locomotives in any numbers it was realised that special facilities would be required for their erection and painting. However, building completely new facilities at main works was never within the BR budget so it was a matter of altering what already existed and making do. This is the paint shop at Derby in March 1959 where D5013 is undergoing some last minute alterations prior to painting. It appears that the Type 2 has some weathering on its fuel tanks already and it might be that the Bo-Bo has already been road tested whilst wearing a primer coat which wasn't unknown – both Derby and Crewe road tested new diesel locomotives when still in primer, as did some of the private contractors such as Beyer, Peacock. Whilst this Type 2 was being built at Derby, the works was also engaged in building the first ten 'Peaks' not to mention the ongoing manufacture of the 350 h.p. 0-6-0DE shunters. Of course, D1 to D10 took a nearly year to build from laying down the frames to painting the last one ready for traffic. Construction of the Type 2s wasn't much faster – it was all down to supply of certain materials in an age where industry was still recovering from post-war upheavals and shortages. Things did change at Derby for the better and by 1961 they were sometimes churning out the Class 45 'Peaks' at the rate of eight a month! Although the average was more like four.

Derby and the 'Peaks' were synonymous. Designed, built, overhauled and finally scrapped there. Perhaps that description did not appl[y]
100% to every one of the 193 locomotives we regarded as 'Peaks' but all were maintained at Derby and more than half were actually bui[lt]
there, however, only twenty-odd met their end at the works. For more than twenty years the big diesels plied their trade over the main line[s]
that were planned, built and run by the powers at Derby. The connection was – one and the same! This is D74 or rather 74 inside one o[f]
the workshops in August 1974. Now this particular 'Peak' was not one of the Derby-built examples but you can forgive the compiler tha[t]
bit of license surely? No.74 became 45051 in January 1975. This Crewe built machine started life at Crewe North in November 1960 b[ut]
was soon transferred to Cricklewood but when this scene was captured on film it was a Toton engine. Its demise came in April 1987 whil[st]
on the strength of Tinsley – not a bad innings really for a supposedly clumsy, heavy and large diesel locomotive. *D.H.Beecroft.*

Taking part in the Works Open Day at Derby in August 1974, a 350 h.p. 0-6-0DE No.08152 looks rather smart in its new blue livery, after completion of a major overhaul. A stranger from the Southern Region and based at Selhurst depot, the presence of this shunter at Derby would have brightened some young enthusiasts' day. Originally (D)3220, this locomotive was built at Darlington in April 1955 as 13220 (renumbered October 1958 to D3220). Condemned in July 1980 – this would have been its last major overhaul – it was towed to Swindon dump where it was swiftly despatched after arrival. This '08' spent the whole of its life working from Selhurst depot. *D.H.Beecroft.*

As mentioned previously the Midland Lines allocated BRC&W Type 2 (TOPS Class 27) had their heavy maintenance taken care of at Derby and in this January 1971 photograph we have No.5413 posing outside the shops on a crisp but bright Saturday afternoon. The external condition of the Bo-Bo is exemplary and besides losing its 'D' prefix, the Type 2 now sports a rail blue livery with the BR double arrow symbol, along with the TOPS classification information box on the lower bodyside where it could be read by interested parties. Of course, this locomotive and all its sisters were now allocated to the Scottish Region at either Eastfield, Haymarket or Inverness – 5413 was in fact a Haymarket charge. So, the question is – what was this '27' doing at Derby works on this date when maintenance of the class had already passed to St Rollox works in Glasgow? The answer was that 5413 and a number of the '27s' were being equipped for push-pull working (that is a locomotive at each end of a set of six air-braked Mark II coaches which had been specially fitted with disc brakes of the Edinburgh (Waverley) – Glasgow (Queen Street) passenger services which were to be accelerated during 1971. The Class 27 was rated to 90 m.p.h. as against 75 m.p.h. with the Class 26. Also receiving attention at Derby during December 1970 and January 1971 were Nos.5404, 5407, 5408, 5409, 5411. Already equipped for multiple-unit working, the locomotives designated for the new task had a number of modifications carried out including the fitting of electrical heating equipment and the removal of the original steam generator, the latter replaced by a diesel powered alternator. Dual-braking equipment, and a communication system linking the cabs and the train guard was also fitted. Derby eventually converted twenty-four of the class whilst St Rollox rebuilt another twelve. Although the accelerated workings were fraught at various times with problems mainly concerning the locomotives, the converted locomotives coped with the high speed running and served the two cities until 1979 when Class 47 powered trains took over the workings. 5413 was renumbered 27118 in November 1973 under the TOPS scheme. Then, in April 1975 it was renumbered again, this time to 27103. Finally, some ten years later was renumbered yet again! It became 27047 in July 1985 and was withdrawn the following 'April at Inverness. Ironically, this particular '27' was afterwards transported all the way to Leicester where it was cut up at the Vic Berry yard in 1987. *D.H.Beecroft.*

Having just undergone a complete overhaul, 46030 is now ready for a visit to the paint shop at Derby works in August 1974. One of the Gateshead allocation, renumbering from (D)167 had taken place at Gateshead depot during the previous February. They might not have been the longest of the pioneer Type 4s at 67ft 11in. (that title went to the EE Type 4 at 69ft 6in.), but the 'Peaks were certainly the heaviest at 138 tons! *D.H.Beecroft.*

The ill-fated 'Fell' diesel in Klondyke sidings at Derby works in early 1960. Having resided here since withdrawal in November 1958, th 4-8-4 (2-D-2) diesel – numbered 10100 but not obvious from this illustration – had been slowly dismantled. The four 500 h.p. Paxman engines, two situated in each nose section, had already been taken out for salvage whilst one of the water tanks for the train heating boiler occupies the nearest engine compartment. When it was released to the world officially in 1952 the locomotive was regarded by man as rather ugly; now it was simply a mess. Although somewhat different from other diesel locomotive designs in having a multi-engine layout – six in all including two auxiliary engines – the 'Fell' proved to be quite reliable but it was different and therefore non-standard It became a regular performer over the line from Derby to Manchester (Central) during the years from 1955, when it was taken into BI stock, to 1958 and on occasion worked the Manchester expresses from St Pancras. However, a fire in one of its two heating boilers, whils it was heading a Derby train at Manchester on 16th October 1958, brought it to a premature end; although how much longer it would hav been in service is debatable anyway. Designed as a 4-8-4, No.10100 ran as a 4-4-4-4 (2-B-B-2) from July 1954 when the central sections o the connecting rods were removed after alterations to the chassis. Weighing in at 120 tons, the locomotive was quite capable of hauling twelve coach passenger train through the Peak District. Behind is another 'prototype' design, the North British Locomotive Co., Paxma powered Bo-Bo No.10800 which, by now, was another withdrawn unit having been in traffic for BR since November 1950. The NBL diese had a somewhat chequered career also and was tried on the LMR, Southern and Eastern Regions working secondary passenger and freigh services. In April 1958 it was 'stored' on the Klondyke until officially withdrawn in August 1959. In 1961 No.10800 taken into the shops a Derby and stripped of its prime mover and generator after which it was taken to the Brush factory at Loughborough to be used as a testin unit. The locomotive was then sold to Brush who re-equipped 10800 with new internal bits - Maybach engine, Brush alternator and tractio motors. A considerable amount of rebuilding was required to fit all the parts into the existing body shell before it went into testing trial By 1968 its testing days were over and afterwards it lay in the yard at Loughborough until scrapped in 1976. *David Dalton.*

The 'Fell' at Derby on 26th May 1957, resplendent in lined green livery and with a newly applied BR crest. The exhaust at the top centre of the body was for one of the 150 h.p. AEC auxiliary engines. The exhaust from the larger Paxman engines came out from four pipes situated at each corner of the roof, just behind and above the cab doors. Unlike the usual diesel locomotive cab doors, the doors on 10100 opened outwards, a bit like a road lorry, because the shafts linking the main engines to the hydraulic couplings and other pipes inhibited inward opening; the crew seats themselves were also immediately inside and adjacent to the doors. The lower illustration shows the 4-4-4-4 with cab doors open, outside the erecting shop at Derby on an unknown date but post July 1954. Note the Ashford-built Bulleid 0-6-0 diesel mechanical shunter – No.11001 – alongside, with its cab section sheeted over! Interesting times the Fifties' and Sixties' on British Railways. *both David Dalton.*

Metro-Vick D5705, along with D5707, share the shed yard with a 'Jubilee' and all the trappings of steam locomotion at Derby in September 1959. Not quite ten months old, this Bo-Co is already looking tired and thoroughly dirty but being stabled amongst steam locomotives at a busy depot was not going to help matters. Derby shed has at least acknowledged the presence of the twenty Type 2s by painting the 17A code on the front bufferbeam. However, when it came to producing pollution, the two-stroke V-8 Crossley engines used by these ninety seven ton monsters had to be seen to be believed; the noise too was hardly friendly to the ears and this compiler remembers their visits to Manchester (Central) station being noisy and smoky affairs even when running light. Now, not being one to promote superstition and the like, it nevertheless seems these ill-fated locomotives did not have a good start because the British Railways crest transfers supplied to the makers had the 'wrong facing' lion and wheel! They should have been facing left but instead they were all facing right! Was that an omen of things to come? Perhaps not because some of the transfers supplied to Vulcan Foundry for fixing to the EE Type 1 were 'wrong facing' too and we all know what happened to that class! Of all the Class 28 diesels, this particular example faired the best in being taken into Departmental use after withdrawal in September 1968. The other nineteen were cut up during 1968 and 1969 by two of the most prolific scrapyards in the country – Cashmore's at Great Bridge who dealt with eleven, and J.McWilliam at Shettleston who got rid of the rest. Ironically, most of these Co-Bos were cut up before many of the steam locomotives which they had been built to replace! D5705 is now privately preserved. The Co-Bos were different – radically so – but from an operating point of view they were basically rubbish.

Destined for the Western Region, 'Peak' D117 draws away from the Up marshalling yard and gains the Up goods on the main line towards Trent at the south end of the Toton complex in June 1969. The train – 8V54 – is made up of vacuum fitted 21-ton hopper wagons loaded with domestic coal. These vehicles are branded **HOUSE COAL CONCENTRATION** and would be destined for one of the dedicated depots scattered about the country. In the right distance can be seen an 0-6-0 diesel shunter working the Chilwell group of sidings, whilst nearer the camera is another 0-6-0DE shunter working the wagon works sidings; the works themselves can be seen behind the Toton Junction signal box. Toton employed a small army of these six-coupled shunting locomotives, its first allocation consisted of five jack-shaft drive types which arrived new from Derby in 1939. What of our subject locomotive D117. This 1-Co-Co-1 arrived new in the area in September 1961 from Crewe. Derby was its first depot but Toton took up its maintenance once the newly built diesel depot was fully commissioned in May 1965. The 'Peak' became 45130 in June 1974 by which time it was fitted with electric train heating and classified 45/1 for Midland main line work. Exactly thirteen years later, whilst allocated to Tinsley, where many of the Toton lot were cascaded to, it was condemned and stood for a number of years awaiting a buyer in the run-down Tinsley marshalling yard. Prior to withdrawal, the 'Peak' was for some reason unofficially named NEWMARKETEER by Tinsley depot. A picture from this same spot today would reveal lines of stored Class 60 locomotives with around 80% of the fleet laid-up in the underused yard. Despite being only about twenty years old, it is unlikely that any of the class rusting here will work again. *D.H.Beecroft.*

A nice view of 45109 (ex D85), heading north through Long Eaton in September 1974, with a train of British Steel Tubes Division hopper wagons. Compare this view with the previous one taken five years earlier from the same position. Now the Toton Junction signal box is gone, as have the semaphore signals. The track appears to have been altered slightly too but the yards, and the wagon shops, seem as busy as ever. Nowadays the wagon shops have been disused for years and partially burnt out through vandalism. Much of the area to the right is now a semi-mature forest. There were plans put forward to create a rail freight hub in the Toton area but it came to nothing due to local opposition on environmental grounds. A lack of decent road access was one reason cited besides the fact that some of Toton yard apparently lies within a green belt area! The A52 dual carriageway bridge passes across the northern throat of the yard whilst the M1 motorway junction is less than half a mile from that same bridge. However, housing developments have risen on areas which were once fields – different priorities are being employed here methinks! 45109 was another ETH 45/1 – a truly mixed traffic class. *D.H.Beecroft.*

Heading for Didcot power station with over a thousand tons of coal, 47199 leaves the Up yard in September 1974 with a train of thirty-four HAA hoppers. The base load installation at Didcot was not yet fully commissioned – that was still some months away – but it was still requiring one of these trains every two hours to satisfy the appetite of the boilers and the stacking ground. Of course not all of Didcot's fuel needs were supplied from the Nottinghamshire coalfield, other areas also sent train loads too, including the South Wales, West Midlands and Yorkshire, the latter trains also streaming through Toton. At this time over 64 million tons of coal was being carried by BR for power station use alone. Coal was still big business and Toton was still playing a leading role in its distribution even though the merry-go-round principle was designed to cut out marshalling yards and wagon sorting. What Toton effectively did – such as it had done since opening – was bring together small train loads to make up bulk loads such as this for onward transit to distant destinations. In principle, pairs of Class 20s brought the trains from the pitheads to the yard and Class 47s took over for the majority of the main line journey. Didcot was just one customer. Down the line to the south was Ratcliffe-on-Soar, another base load power station, which demanded similar tonnage's of coal to Didcot and it too was supplied in part through Toton although some trains passed right through the yard being direct pit to power station workings – true MGR. Having transferred from Crewe to Toton in May 1973 as (D)1849, this Co-Co was renumbered in march 1974. Returning to Crewe in February 1976, 47199 was condemned there in August 1987 but not broken up until December 1993. *D.H.Beecroft.* 45

Another Class 8 train leaves Toton yard in September 1974 although the view of most of the stock is obliterated by the smoke-screen generated by 'Peak' 134 as it sweeps onto the Nottingham line. *D.H.Beecroft.*

Looking north in April 1975, the photographer is standing at the outlet to a wagon repair shop at Long Eaton, situated immediately south of Toton marshalling yard. The main subject of the picture is, perhaps, the northbound empty MGR headed by 45054. But the bulk of the frame is filled by the bridge through which the camera is pointing. The bridge itself spans the main line and is supporting the two arrival roads for the Down marshalling yard. On the nearest road can be seen another train of empty wagons, these bound for sorting in the Down yard at Toton prior to onward transit to the collieries. The bridge dates from about 1899 when expansion of the existing yards at Toton saw this structure erected to eliminate conflicting movements on the main line whereby previously two-thirds of the trains destined for the Down yard on the west side of the Erewash valley line originated from routes on the east side of that line. In the background is the footbridge from where a number of the illustrations in this album were captured on film. This picture also provides an interesting contrast in mineral wagons with the soon to be obsolete square-bodied, unfitted, 16-ton variety on the bridge above, and the relatively modern air braked 32-ton hoppers behind the 'Peak'. *D.H.Beecroft.*

Besides its 'Peaks', Brush Type 4s, and complement of Sulzer Type 2s, Toton was renowned for its large fleet of English Electric Type 1s – the 20s – which usually worked in pairs, coupled front-to-front giving the driver an uninterrupted view of the road ahead. However D8088, seen here on the fuelling roads at Toton, is bucking that trend and appears to be working solo albeit with a brake tender coupled. The date is May 1970, a time when much of the coal traffic handled by the Toton fleet was still carried in unfitted mineral wagons hence the requirement of extra braking capacity, especially on some of the colliery branches, where this class was employed. Eventually the brake tenders would become redundant as BR fitted more stock with air brakes but that took some years to complete and during the interim period the 20s worked more and more in pairs, not only for the extra braking but because the trains themselves were getting heavier too. Much of the shed at Toton forms the background to this illustration and it is worth recalling the layout of the building. We are situated at the north-east corner of the fifteen-road shed with the nearest four roads dedicated to everyday servicing; those roads were carried right through the shed allowing locomotives to queue-up and exit without conflicting movements. The following eight roads, which were dead-ended, consisted the maintenance section. The final three roads, note the higher roof profile, contained the heavy maintenance area where locomotives could be lifted off their bogies with jacks. A 4-ton capacity overhead crane spanned all three of the heavy maintenance roads and was available to lift large engine components. Toton was reputed to be the biggest diesel depot in Western Europe when it was opened and that claim has never been challenged. Even today Toton has a large fleet of locomotives to look after and the heaviest of repairs are still carried out within that western section of the building. It was certainly a very busy depot in 1970 and nowadays it plays a major role in keeping the locomotive fleets of the privatised railways maintained. *D.H.Beecroft.*

line-up of 'Peaks' outside the servicing shed in May 1970. A respectable looking Class 45, No.84 ROYAL CORPS OF TRANSPORT waits entry; as 45055, this Type 4 was withdrawn in April 1985. Alongside is one of the original 'Peaks' soon to be Class 44, with its four-disc headcode and connecting doors. Note that each of the shed roads are numbered. *D.H.Beecroft.*

Class 20s everywhere! Toton certainly was the centre of the Class 20 universe. The accompanying allocation list from the first day of 197
shows more that a hundred of these useful English Electric Type 1s were 'shedded' at Toton for maintenance. This is D8150 in June 1970
standing alone on the Sand road, with the fuelling roads adjacent, awaiting further duties. Although a vast number of the 20s were unde
the care of Toton, it was rare to find more than thirty of them 'on shed' even at weekends because they were at various stabling and fuellin
points throughout the Nottingham Division. The ability of the diesel locomotive to be switched on and off, as simply as that, enabled BI
to leave locomotives switched off, and often unattended, at stabling points overnight and especially at weekends. As already mentioned
Toton had a number of these stabling points under its 'jurisdiction' and a visit to two of them on Sunday 28th March 1971, found th
following Class 20s, all coupled in pairs: Coalville – 8009+8040, 8067+8183, 8145+8152, 8155+8193, 8176+8198, 8184+8189; besides these
two of Toton's 47s, 1809 and 1810, were also present. At the old Westhouses engine shed, by then roofless, which had taken on some of th
duties previously worked by Kirkby-in-Ashfield (closed October 1970), the number of 20s stabled was somewhat greater, all were couple
in pairs for multiple working: 8006+8197, 8011+8134, 8014+8185, 8081+8182, 8125+8180, 8138+8194, 8146+8179, 8156+8163, 8168+817:
Two more of Toton's 47s were also at this location in the shape of 1805 and 1810. During one weekend in October 1969 Kirkby stablin
point had seventeen pairs of Class 20s resident – thirty-four locomotives of the same class! Finally, regarding this particular view of Toto
shed, the single road section of the building immediately behind the locomotive was the wheel lathe; the wagons loaded with swarfe givin
a clue as to the activities inside. *D.H.Beecroft.*

TOTON ALLOCATION - 1st January 1972 - Probably at its peak!

Class 08:
3021, 3026, 3029, 3036, 3037, 3039, 3044, 3056, 3058, 3249, 3340, 3345, 3362, 3363, 3390, 3400, 3402, 3404, 3505, 3514, 3777, 3789, 3852, 3996, 3997.

Class 20:
8002, 8003, 8006, 8009, 8011, 8012, 8013, 8014, 8015, 8016, 8035, 8036, 8037, 8038, 8039, 8040, 8042, 8043, 8044, 8045, 8047, 8062, 8063, 8064, 8066, 8067, 8068, 8069, 8070, 8071, 8072, 8073, 8074, 8075, 8076, 8077, 8081, 8083, 8087, 8088, 8111, 8114, 8115, 8122, 8134, 8135, 8136, 8137, 8138, 8139, 8140, 8141, 8142, 8143, 8144, 8145, 8146, 8147, 8148, 8149, 8150, 8151, 8152, 8153, 8154, 8155, 8156, 8157, 8158, 8159, 8160, 8161, 8162, 8163, 8164, 8165, 8166, 8167, 8168, 8169, 8170, 8171, 8172, 8173, 8174, 8175, 8176, 8177, 8178, 8179, 8180, 8181, 8182, 8183, 8184, 8185, 8186, 8187, 8188, 8189, 8190, 8191, 8192, 8193, 8194, 8195, 8196, 8197, 8198, 8199.

Class 25:
5224, 5225, 5226, 5227, 5228, 5229, 5230, 5231, 5232, 5233, 5234, 5235, 5236, 5237, 5238, 5239, 5240, 5241, 5242, 5243, 5244, 5246, 5247, 5248, 5249, 5250, 5266, 5267, 5268, 5269, 5270, 7500, 7501, 7502, 7503, 7504, 7505, 7506, 7507, 7508, 7509, 7510, 7511, 7512, 7513, 7514, 7515, 7516, 7517, 7518, 7519, 7520, 7521, 7522, 7523, 7524, 7558, 7559, 7560, 7561, 7562, 7563, 7564, 7604, 7605, 7606, 7607, 7608, 7620, 7626, 7647, 7649, 7651.

Class 44:
1, 2, 3, 4, 5, 6, 7, 8, 9, 10.

Class 45:
11, 29, 32, 33, 35, 36, 37, 38, 39, 40, 41, 42, 43, 44, 45, 46, 47, 48, 49, 50, 51, 52, 54, 55, 56, 57, 58, 59, 61, 62, 63, 64, 65, 66, 67, 68, 69, 70, 71, 72, 73, 74, 75, 76, 77, 78, 79, 80, 81, 82, 83, 84, 85, 86, 87, 88, 90, 91, 92, 93, 94, 95, 96, 97, 98, 99, 100, 101, 102, 103, 104, 105, 106, 107, 108, 109, 110, 111, 113, 114, 115, 116, 117, 118, 119, 120, 121, 122, 123, 124, 125, 126, 127, 128, 130, 131, 132, 133, 134, 135, 136, 137.

Class 47:
1540, 1544, 1616, 1622, 1623, 1633, 1634, 1801, 1802, 1803, 1804, 1805, 1806, 1807, 1809, 1810, 1825, 1826, 1827, 1828, 1829, 1830, 1831, 1832, 1833, 1834, 1854, 1855, 1856, 1960, 1961.

Total: 353.

The situation was similar in the summer of 1968 except that the BRC&W Type 2s, Classes 26 and 27, were quite prolific in England then, and especially so in the Nottingham Division where the following were to be found allocated to Toton for maintenance: D5370 to D5382, D5384 to D5399, D5409 to D5415. Of course from July onwards these later all transferred to the Scottish Region swapped, in the main, for EE Type 1s, and some Derby Sulzer Type 2s. By 1971 standardisation was certainly beginning to take effect!

TOTON'S OWN 'PEAKS' – Class 44:

Class leader: D1 SCAFELL PIKE on the fuelling roads at Toton in August 1969. Virtually unchanged, livery-wise, since its trip on 21st April 1959, from Derby works to St Pancras for inspection by British Transport Commission members. Afterwards road and load testing occupied D1 until it was eventually released to traffic in mid-August working, appropriately, from Derby shed. The naming had been carried out beforehand, by the Lord Lieutenant of Cumberland at Carlisle Citadel station on 14th July. Initially on crew training runs prior to the introduction of further 'Peaks' in September, D1 worked the occasional express passenger service over different parts of the Midland Lines. In April 1960 it was transferred to Camden, thence to Longsight in May for a two-year stint at 9A. In March 1962, its job on the WCML complete, it moved back to the Midland Lines and was allocated to Toton where the steam roundhouses offered the only accommodation until the diesel depot was built a couple of years in the future. Ten years in traffic had seen a few changes to the big diesels' appearance. The broad off-white stripe which was painted along the lower body (hereafter called a cheat line), just above the sill and between the cab doors, has been painted over in the same colour green as the rest of the body. A yellow warning panel graces the front plate now whilst a TOPS information panel – just discernible – is positioned beneath the number by the driver's door at the No.1 end. In the first few months of 1969 all ten of the class were apparently put into store but why that event took place is unknown. During a works visit from September to November 1971 blue livery was applied and D1 became simply 1. Under TOPS, No.1 became 44001 on 27th February 1974 with the renumbering taking place at Toton depot. Withdrawn on the penultimate day of October 1976, SCAFELL PIKE was cut up at its birth place during February 1977. *D.H.Beecroft*.

The afternoon sun of a glorious June day in 1970 reveals the less than pristine green livery worn by D2 HELVELLYN whilst it stands on the fuelling roads on the east side of Toton shed. Sister engine D9 SNOWDON is queuing behind. Note that the off-white body stripe on D2 remains untouched but spillage, and a certain amount of scouring from the washing plant, spoils the near original finish. This 'Peak' was the last one of the class to settle down at Toton and was finally transferred in August 1962 from Crewe although it had initially arrived at Toton in March of that year before being called back to the WCML in June. Like D1, D2 was allocated to Derby and was put into traffic on 19th September 1959. During the following May it moved to Edge Hill but then transferred to Camden two months later and from where it worked until March 1962; it had apparently been working from Camden throughout the winter of 1959/60. From September 1959 to 1963, D2 had been experimentally up-rated from 2300 h.p. to 2500 h.p. to gain experience prior to D11 to D193 entering service. A works visit during April and May 1972 saw blue paint applied whilst renumbering to 44002 was carried out at Toton on Tuesday 19th March 1974. Withdrawn in February 1979, 44002 was cut up at Derby during the following October. Unlike D1, D2, along with the other eight members of the class, had been named at Derby works prior to entering service and it was an exhibit at the works annual Flower Show on Saturday 29th August. The depot water tank and the fuel tanks form the background whilst in the distance is the hill known locally as 'Toton bank' from where a good view of the yard and depot activities could be had. A visit today will reveal the depot in all its glory but many of the locomotives are stored, even the modern classes, whilst the massive marshalling yard is virtually derelict – a reflection, perhaps, of Britain's onetime industrial might. *D.H.Beecroft.*

It is still June 1970 but late in the evening as D3 SKIDDAW joins the queue outside the servicing shed at Toton. Entering traffic on the same day as D2, this 'Peak' also moved across to the LMR Western Lines working initially from Camden but settling down at Crewe until its terminal transfer to Toton in March 1962. A shadow of the lower body cheat line shows through the worn and stained paintwork. It was to be May 1973 before this locomotive was painted in blue livery; by which time this green livery would have looked completely 'washed out' unless patching had been carried out. Note the letter M beneath the fleet number, denoting Midland Lines. The others previously illustrated also carried that designation at this period. Once again D9 is trying to get into the picture from the rear. *D.H.Beecroft.*

aiting to proceed off shed in August 1974, 44003 looks rather splendid compared to the way it was depicted in the previous illustration. inted blue in May 1973, the renumbering was performed at Toton on 10th March 1974. Whilst attending Derby works for assessment, 003 became the first of the original 'Peaks' to be withdrawn, the event taking place at Klondyke sidings on Saturday 17th July 1976, some ur years before the total demise of the class. It was cut up during the following week at Derby where it was created less than eighteen ars previously. Note that the connecting doors in the nose sections of most of these pioneer 1-Co-Co-1s were welded up during the 'Toton ars' but those on 44003 still appear to be operative - a bit of a draught would therefore be prevalent for most of the time. *D.H.Beecroft.*

D4 GREAT GABLE outside the servicing shed in June 1969. This was the first of the class to be given blue livery, the repaint bein performed during a visit to Derby as early as the period December 1966 to February 1967. Of course, then, it came out complete wit the prefix to its number as here. It was also given a small yellow panel at each end whereas now the larger version of that warning devic has been applied. The bodywork, in just over two years, has deteriorated somewhat, even the lettering on the nameplate looks rath anonymous. Completed and entering traffic on 26th September 1959, D4 followed the first three locomotives to Camden and resid there officially for two years before transferring direct to Toton in March 1962. First at one thing, last with another - GREAT GABL was the last to be renumbered and it became 44004 at Toton on Monday 8th April 1974. Withdrawn in November 1980, amongst th final three survivors, this 'Peak' has been preserved, repainted to its original green livery and renumbered to D4. Today it resides, mo appropriately, at the Midland Railway Centre, Butterley. *(opposite, top)* D5 CROSS FELL with D7 outside the shed at Toton in August 196 The cheat line has gone, a yellow warning panel has been applied along with the TOPS information panel but otherwise everything is th same as built. *(opposite, bottom)* As simply number 5 outside the wheel lathe shed in July 1973. A fountain of exhaust, which is more tha just a tick-over, is discernible so perhaps our subject was undergoing an engine test of sorts. Judging by the amount of soot staining o the wall behind No.5, this area of the depot must have been used for running-up the engines after attention. The cables draped alongsid and over the roof of the shed carried current for the wheel lathe during a period of National power cuts imposed in 1973 by the the Tory Government. Having the means to overcome power shortages, Toton depot located a '44' or '45' on the Stores road at the wester extremity of the shed building to generate electricity whenever the power cuts took affect. This class member was another early recipie of the blue livery, the colour applied at Derby in August 1970. *all D.H.Beecroft.*

(above) Caught once again throwing out a nice bit of exhaust, 44005 is prepared for its next trip in October 1974. Renumbering was carried out on 15th November 1973 during overhaul at Derby. Withdrawn on the final day of April 1978, 44005 was cut up at Derby during the following December. (opposite, top) D6 WHERNSIDE attached to a brake tender at Toton depot in August 1969. This class member managed to clock up more allocations than any of the others, some of the transfers taking place rather late on. From being put into traffic at Camden in mid November 1959, it returned to Derby during December and spent the next six months at 17A. Then it was off to Carlisle Upperby with D5 for a near two-year stay although D5 had gone back to Camden in July 1960. Arriving at Toton in March 1962 WHERNSIDE then moved back to Derby in April and over to Saltley in June. In July it returned to Toton ready for the great gathering which took place in August with the arrival of D2. Note the paint 'splodges' applied to the same strategic areas on each bogie – no doubt a method used to spot any fractures or fatigue at known vulnerable spots. (opposite, bottom) One year later, in July 1970, and D6 now has a full frontal yellow warning panel which appears to be freshly applied whilst the bogies have themselves been given a clean and a fresh coat of paint. The rest of the body has been treated to nothing more than a patch-up and most of that was to eradicate the cheat line. D6 had just completed a period of overhaul at Derby. The first of he class to be renumbered in the Class 44 series, D6 became 44006 on October 1973 whilst undergoing another overhaul at Derby. At the same time it lost its green livery. Withdrawal took place on 25th January 1977 and 44006 was broken up shortly afterwards. all D.H.Beecroft.

D7 INGLEBOROUGH on 7th June 1970. The Toton 'painters' have been busy obliterating the cheat line and covering up the plated-over footholds behind the cab door. Careful perusal will see that the 'D' has also been painted out in the recent paint-fest. All-over green is the order of the day now until the next works visit. With the heating boiler either removed or isolated there is no further need for the second man to scale the bodyside to 'put the bag in.' D7, like the rest of the pioneer 'Peaks' went initially to work on the West Coast Main Line at Camden, in December 1959 it slipped away to Derby until the following April went it returned to Camden. In March 1962, with plenty of English Electric Type 4s available for the Anglo-Scottish route, D7 transferred to Toton. *D.H.Beecroft.*

By October 1974 INGLEBOROUGH had its TOPS number 44007, double-arrow symbols and a coat of blue paint. Renumbering actually took place on 27th February 1974 whilst the blue livery was applied at Derby in February 1973. Entering service in November 1959, withdrawal took place in November 1980. When introduced onto the Toton-Washwood Heath loose-coupled coal trains in 1962, the ten original 'Peaks' had a part in revolutionising that traffic in order to speed up passenger workings over the main line to Birmingham. By the end of 1962 the ten Type 4s, with a little help from odd members of the 2,500 h.p. variety of the class, were completing some forty-seven return workings a week – eight a day, with Saturday fluctuations – between the two centres. It was possible for crews to undertake out and home working in a single shift thereby creating a greater efficiency in men and machines. Because of its somewhat easier graded line, the route from Toton to Birmingham did not require the diesels to use brake tenders whereas on the route south to Wellingborough and London, brake tenders became a necessary provision with loose-coupled mineral trains. It was reported that during their stand-over period between working the Washwood Heath traffic, D1 to D10 undertook further coal train haulage to the power stations at Castle Donnington, Drakelow and Willington. *D.H.Beecroft.*

The water tanks which once hung beneath the body, between the bogies, were removed a couple of years after the class arrived at Toton - probably when the new maintenance shed was fully commissioned - and coincided with the removal of the heating boilers. It has been intimated that the heating boilers, at least on some members of the class – D1, D6, D7, D8 and D9 – were removed during a visit to Crewe works undertaken by those mentioned in December 1961 and February 1962. This is D8 PENYGHENT waiting to enter the maintenance shed at Toton in August 1969 along with sister D5 CROSS FELL. Except for the erstwhile water tanks, and the yellow warning panel on the front plate, the 1-Co-Co-1 is very much the same as it was when it entered traffic at Camden shed on 28th December 1959. It too had a spell at Derby from January to May 1960 but went back to the WCML and was allocated to Crewe North. But in September of that year it was tested with a dynamometer car and a train of fitted mineral wagons between Toton yard and Brent. D8 was in fact the first of the class to transfer permanently to the Midland Lines when in February 1962 it moved to Nottingham shed for a four-month stint prior to joining the bulk of the class at Toton in May. What Nottingham used the big diesel for during that time is unknown but running around some of the freight only lines in the coalfields to check clearances might have been part of the reason for its short stay. Blue livery was applied in July 1971 and renumbering took place on 7th March 1974. Note that the TOPS information panel has recently been applied next to the driver's door. As 44008, this 'Peak' was amongst the final trio which were all withdrawn in November 1980. *D.H.Beecroft.*

44008 looking rather smart – at least above the bogies – in April 1975. The nameplates are still in situ but considering these pioneer 'Peaks' rarely worked north of Leeds anymore, the names could be regarded as superfluous. Nevertheless, the 44s were kept busy with freight duties and even the occasional enthusiasts' railtour. The latter work became a regular weekend job for the survivors in 1977. On 21st January 1978 this locomotive, along with sister 44009 which did the first stint from Nottingham to Crewe via the Woodhead route, worked back to Nottingham from Crewe via Chester, Shrewsbury, Wolverhampton, Walsall and Burton. The railtour turned out to be the last that any of the class would be involved in. Serious inroads were now being made into the class as Derby scrapyard beckoned but 44008 was to escape into the world of preservation after being withdrawn in November 1980. Today it resides at Peak Rail, Matlock – another very appropriate location for a 'Peak'. *D.H.Beecroft.*

(above) The cheat line on D9 SNOWDON has been eradicated by a more professional hand and was probably done at main works or by a more sympathetic hand at Toton. The hand/foot holds are still open but this is June 1970 and radical changes were about to take place. But radical changes had already taken place with this '44' in the shape of the headcode which was fitted in 1969 after collision damage necessitated a complete replacement nose section following an incident at Trent in 1968 – it was the only one of the original ten to carry such. Ironically the headcode 8F79 sums up the lot of the original 'Peaks' by now – Class 8 freight haulage. *(below)* For want of a better word, the 'grillage' on the bodyside of 44009, and 44010 too, was somewhat different from that worn by the rest of the class and looked like, well, security fencing! It is August 1974 and 44009 appears for all the world like a '46'. Renumbering had been taken care of at Toton on 16th February last whilst the blue livery was applied during a works visit to Derby in March 1972. *both D.H.Beecroft.*

(*above*) The other side of SNOWDON, in September 1974, showing that the austere 'grillage' was fitted to both sides of the body. This is more or less 44009 in its final form. Released to traffic on 26th December 1959 (in the days when many people worked on Boxing Day, especially the railways), D9 went straight to Camden but was apparently transferred to Derby in the New Year only to return to 1B in February 1960. During the following May it settled down at Edge Hill until the call from Toton beckoned. Not amongst the lucky ones, and because of its different No.1 front end making it an unlikely candidate for preservation, 44009 was condemned in March 1979 but was not broken up until July 1980. Notice the rather pathetic sign on the shed cladding between 8 and 9 roads proclaiming that this was TOTON. (*below*) D10 TRYFAN, minus nameplate, gracing Toton depot yard in August 1969. The last of the pilot scheme 'Peaks' D10 was put into traffic on 6th February 1960 at Camden. Derby shed used it during March 1960 and in that time it was prepared to be exhibited at St Pancras station on Monday the 21st for the benefit of the Transport Minister, one Ernest Marples (probably the most fervent of the anti-rail ministers from any Tory Government in post-war history) before releasing it to Camden shed once again. However, during the following May, D10 was transferred to Crewe from where it worked until March 1962 when it joined the others at Toton for their new role – hauling slow and heavy freight trains. Blue livery was applied in December 1972 and renumbering was carried out on 26th February 1974 at Toton. *both D.H.Beecroft.*

44010 minus nameplate in September 1974. It became normal practice to remove the nameplates from the class from about this time for security reasons after a series of thefts throughout BR but in the case of 44010 it seems that the plates had not been re-fixed since its 1969 photograph. Whenever any '44' was involved in a railtour or such, the plates were refitted for the occasion otherwise they were locked away at Toton. Waiting to go off shed – the 10 m.p.h. notice was for road vehicles – 44010 had less than two and a half years of service left before it was condemned on 26th May 1977 (it had been withdrawn initially on 18th September 1976 but was re-instated six weeks on 31st October). 44010's premature end came about on 11th May 1977 when, whilst working a coal train near Mansfield Junction, it caught fire. Hauled back to Toton, it was assessed as a write-off and condemned. On 18th June it was taken to Derby works but was towed back to Toton on 16th August so that any useful parts could be cannibalised. Eventually, on 10th February 1978 it was taken to Derby for the final time (in special freight 9X49) and was completely cut up in July. *D.H.Beecroft.*

At the end of August 1974 one of Longsight's Class 40 fleet paid a visit to Toton on an unknown working. 40003 in immaculate condition, actually ex Crewe works after a heavy overhaul and repaint. Renumbered from 203 during the previous March, this locomotive was one of the ten of the original Eastern Region batch which introduced the English Electric Type 4 to the world. Stratford was its first allocation and from where it worked the accelerated Liverpool Street-Norwich expresses. When the Great Eastern lines eventually got their allocation of the Brush Type 4s the Stratford based EE Type 4s, D200 to D209, transferred to the Western Lines of the London Midland Region. This particular locomotive ended its working days hauling freight from Healey Mills and was withdrawn in September 1982. Doncaster works, where this locomotive was first accepted from Vulcan Foundry by British Railways in May 1958, had the job of cutting up the 133 ton hulk in 1984. *D.H.Beecroft.*

Not having any Class 46 'Peaks' of its own any more, Toton only ever saw the Gateshead based members of the class when they worked into the East Midlands on parcels or freight trains. The last allocated '46' was D147 which left for Bristol at the end of 1971. This is a rather clean 46050 (Gateshead's reputation in steam days for putting dirty locomotives into traffic had obviously been buried since mechanical washing plant had been installed at GD) outside Toton's servicing shed in September 1974. Besides Gateshead, the only other depots with an allocation of Class 46 at this period were both on the Western Region, at Bristol Bath Road and Plymouth Laira. Outwardly the Class 46 was no different than Class 45 but internally they had different traction motors and generators which had been supplied by Brush rather than the Crompton Parkinson equipment on the 45s. All of the 46s were built at Derby whereas the building of the 45s was shared between Crewe and Derby with the former workshop having the lions' share. One other item of note was the fact that none of the 46s had split head codes. Towards the end of their working lives the members of Class 46 were allocated to just two depots, Gateshead which maintained the bulk of the class, and Laira where a handful remained until December 1980. That particular date turned out to be significant for the class as a whole when twenty-three of the fifty-one survivors were withdrawn en masse. However, less than twelve months later seventeen of those had been re-instated to traffic, some for a few months but most for a couple of years or until the complete demise of the class in November 1984. 46050 was one of the re-instated locomotives but its final withdrawal took place in October 1982. Like many others of its ilk, it was cut up at Swindon. *D.H.Beecroft.*

The advent of the diesel locomotive on BR meant that motive power no longer worked just within their district or divisional areas and could instead work out of their Region or, as in the case of this Class 37, well beyond even those boundaries going not only out of Region but through another to get to its destination. In October 1974, Eastfield based 37156 had brought freight from Scotland down to the East Midlands by an unknown route but probably via Edinburgh, Newcastle and York. Originally allocated to Landore, near Swansea, as D6856, this Co-Co migrated to Scotland, firstly at Polmadie and then under Eastfield when Polmadie was downgraded to a stabling and fuelling point. Renumbered under TOPS in April 1974, 37156 became 37311 in March 1986 when it was dedicated to the Scottish steel traffic sector. At the same time it was named BRITISH STEEL HUNTERSTON. Reverting to 37156 in September 1989, the locomotive kept the name until October 1994. Withdrawn in June 1999, age 36 years, this Type 3 had certainly paid its way. *D.H.Beecroft.*

This split head code '37' 37025, was a visitor from Thornaby on Teesside and is being prepared to return home in October 1974 after working in on steel traffic from Lackenby. One of the earlier EE Type 3s, it was taken into traffic in August 1961 at Stratford as D672? Becoming 37025 in February 1974, it moved back to the former Great Eastern line in the late Seventies but only as far south as Marc depot. It then went to Scottish Region and was named INVERNESS TMD in March 1994. In was withdrawn in February 1999 at Toton be instead of being sold to one of the scrap metal merchants, it was purchased for preservation and is resident now at Bo' ness as part of the Scottish Class 37 Group collection. The name plates were not removed until two months after withdrawal but were refitted in Septembe 2007 to complement the large logo blue livery with Highland Stag logos on the cab sides. *D.H.Beecroft.*

egular – daily – visitors to Toton were the Class 31s from Tinsley – TI. Indeed, when 31305 was photographed in October 1974, classmate 1227 was close by too. After a change from Mirlees to English Electric prime mover, this class of Brush Type 2s turned out to be another f the success stories of the 1955 Modernisation Plan and more than two-hundred and sixty of them became BR property between ctober 1957 and October 1962. Originally numbered D5838, this locomotive was initially allocated to Darnall in April 1962, when it was t into traffic, but moved across town to Tinsley when the latter depot was commissioned in early 1964. TOPS renumbering was carried ut, like so many others, in February 1974. The first Brush Type 2 to visit Toton depot was D5584 during November and December 1963, hen the March based diesel was apparently 'on loan' to the LMR shed to enable footplate staff to become acquainted with the type in eadiness for their introduction on the through mineral traffic from Wath to Toton whereby Wath-based (Tinsley) locomotives would be sed. Just a few years ago one was tested between Crewe and Derby with a view to them working that service for East Midlands Trains ut although the trials went well the reason for them not being used was given as the inability to maintain time (just) between Stoke and idsgrove where they had to mix with Virgin Pendolinos. The class 153 single-car units now used still struggle to keep time on occasions perhaps there was another reason. *D.H.Beecroft.*

This illustration is included to show what happened at weekends when the bulk of the Toton fleet was stabled and the rest of the railway network was running on half power. The date is 4th May 1968, a Saturday, and we are right on the edge of what was to become the Nottingham Division of BR, at the site of the defunct ex-GNR station called Teversal East. This place is the head of the mile-long branch from Skegby junction and which served the collieries at Silverhill and Teversal, the station was originally provided for miners, though post-WW2 it did provide some excursion traffic to the coast. This particular event is a visit by members of the Stephenson Locomotive Society during a rail tour of the area conducted in two three-car DMUs of which the nearest car was M50325, a Metropolitan-Cammell motor composite. Note that the enthusiasts have been allowed total freedom of the site and were taking advantage of that, as we all did in those heady days before the H&SE existed. The view was captured from the bridge carrying the former Midland (by now freight only) line from Westhouses to Pleasley and Mansfield Woodhouse. That line too had a station at this location also by the name of Teversal but with the suffix Manor; it had closed in July 1930 but like its counterpart below, was used for excursion trains on occasion. At the time of the visit, both collieries previously mentioned were producing in excess of half a million tons of coal each, per year. Silverhill, which can be seen on the left horizon, was opened in 1875 and was in production until 1992. Teversal, out of frame to the right, started producing coal in 1868 and closed in 1980. Both mines were linked underground to Shirebrook, some four miles away to the north-east. The mountains of colliery waste in the background have now either disappeared or been 'softened' so that they blend more into the landscape; such steps have also been taken at other colliery sites too in order to eradicate all remains of an industry which was important to both the railway and the country as a whole. *David Dalton.*